AF480179

The Mystery Of
10,000 LAKES

By Randy Persson

Illustrations by Thomas Rodriguez

INKWELL BOOKS
Writing-Publishing-Printing

ISBN: 978-1-7366445-3-9
Library of Congress Control Number: 2020986432

Published by Inkwell Books LLC
10632 North Scottsdale Road, Unit 695
Scottsdale, AZ 85254
Tel. 480-315-3781
E-mail info@inkwellbooksllc.com
Website www.inkwellbooksllc.com

Dedication

I dedicate this book to the memory of my cousin, Billy Adams (b. 1949, d. 2022.) He passed away just as I was finishing this book and he and his wonderful personality will be missed by all who knew him.

In the attached photo, you see the bench dedicated to my Dad at the Kittson County Veterans Memorial in Lake Bronson, Minnesota. Also in the photo are Cousin Billy (always smiling), his wife Mary, me and my son Drew.

Mysteries are to be explored and memories are to be cherished.

Forward

I am Taylor and me and my brother Drew love solving the mysteries of nature. The first mystery book we wrote was about Montana and *The Mystery of Wildhorse Island*, and the second mystery book was about Arizona and *The Mystery of the Grand Canyon and Climate Change*.

We are a little older now and this book is about our trip to Minnesota to solve the mystery of the 10,000 lakes. We both wondered how there could be 10,000 lakes in one state. We are writing this book with a little help from our dad. His name is Randy.

To add to the mystery of the 10,000 lakes, we found out that there are more than 10,000 lakes in Minnesota! The people of Minnesota are nice, and they don't like to brag so we guessed that they felt 10,000 lakes was more than enough to put on their license plates. They may not like to brag but we can tell you that they do love telling stories!!

We love adventure and especially solving the mysteries of nature. Nature is everywhere and to discover its mysteries is more than fun, it's the best.

Enjoy reading along with us as we discover the lakes, mysteries and tall tales that are Minnesota.

Table of Contents

WELCOME
TO
Minnesota
LAND OF 10,000 LAKES

CHAPTER 1

The Twin Cities

Our adventure began with a direct flight from Phoenix, Arizona to Minneapolis, Minnesota. As the plane began its long descent to land at the airport in Minneapolis, we looked out the window and saw lots of blue water, golden fields of grain, red barns and farmhouses tucked in between tall, beautiful green pine trees.

The airplane touched down on the runway and we took down our backpacks from the overhead bin and headed to the exit door. We stepped off the plane and when we got through the tunnel, we were greeted in the seating area by a big sign that said, "Welcome to the Twin Cities." Our cousins, Madison and Mia, are twins and the sign would certainly catch their attention if they were with us.

"Wow," Drew said, "Does that mean they have cities especially for twins? Maybe Madison and Mia should move here!"

Dad laughed. He explained that the two biggest cities in Minnesota were Minneapolis and St. Paul, and they were right next to each other on different sides of the Mississippi River.

Drew and I looked at each other. "So, does that mean they look exactly alike?" I asked. And dad said, "No, the two cities are similar with only the river between them; however, just like Madison and Mia, they aren't identical and are different in many ways. Minneapolis is the larger city and St. Paul is the capital of Minnesota."

We walked to baggage claim where we met my dad's cousin Billy. Dad and Billy grew up together in northern Minnesota and I could tell they were happy to see each other as they shook hands and hugged each other. Dad is an only child, so Cousin Billy is one of our closest relatives.

"Taylor, Drew, this is my cousin Billy. We played together as kids. He and his wife, Mary, live in Minneapolis. He is going to go with us on our trip. He knows a lot about Minnesota, fishing, and farming, and it will be fun for us to travel with him."

We got our luggage and as we walked through the parking lot, we noticed that the license plates on the Minnesota cars said "10,000 Lakes." "Amazing," Drew and I said at the same time. "That's a lot of lakes!"

"We have more than that," Billy said. "According to the travel books, we have over 15,000 lakes in Minnesota."

"Holy mackerel!" Drew exclaimed and Billy said, "No, mackerel are saltwater fish, Drew. But the freshwater lakes of Minnesota have plenty of walleyes, northern pike, bass, trout, the mighty muskellunge, and many panfish varieties."

My brother started talking about how he would catch one of every type of fish, but I said, "If they have over 15,000 lakes, why do their licenses plates say 10,000?"

Dad shrugged his shoulders. "I don't know, maybe saying 10,000 lakes makes the point that there are a lot of lakes in Minnesota without bragging about so many more."

Being from Arizona, where there are only 156 lakes, Drew and I agreed that if we lived in the middle of 15,000 lakes, we would brag about it to everyone.

Dad knew that we love mysteries—we enjoy trying to figure out things—and that we should try to solve the mystery of how Minnesota got so many lakes.

"Cool beans," I said, and Drew said we should count them.

Dad laughed. "That will keep you both pretty busy for a very long time!"

CHAPTER 2

Lake Minnetonka

We found Cousin Billy's car in the huge airport parking garage and with him as our driver, we drove south and west of Minneapolis to Lake Minnetonka, our first lake in Minnesota.

On the way, Billy explained that Minnesota got its name from the Native American Tribe called the Dakota who lived in this area at least 9,000-12,000 years ago. Minnesota is a Dakota word, and the state is named after the Minnesota River. "Mni" is the Dakota word for water and "Sota" is the Dakota word for "sky-tinted" or "cloudy." One story is that the Dakota women would put milk in the water to explain to settlers the idea of cloudy water. Others say the clay along the Minnesota River is slightly blue, which could explain the "sky-tinted" definition.

"So, the lakes and rivers were here before the Native Americans? Where did they come from?" I asked.

Billy looked in the rear-view mirror at us sitting in the back seat and said, "Yes, it is believed that just after the last ice Age, when all the glaciers that had moved into North America began to melt, the animals and the tribes following them found a land bridge from Siberia to Alaska, in what is now the Aleutian Islands. The tribes hunted the animals such as wooly mammoths and buffalo for food and clothing for their families. Their journey took them through Canada and into northern United States and some tribes even farther south into Mexico and Latin America."

Drew listened patiently to Billy, trying not to interrupt him and then his excitement got the best of him, and he burst out, "Lake Minnetonka? is this lake where they made the yellow Tonka Truck I have at home?"

Dad laughed, "I had a Tonka dump truck when I lived here. "They don't make the trucks and toys on the lake. The original factory was nearby and the company, Tonka, got its name from the Sioux, another Native American tribe, a word meaning 'large.'"

Drew asked, "Since they are so well made, are they made by Minnesota Vikings?"

Again, dad smiled. "Well, Drew, let's say that there is a Viking heritage in Minnesota and that could be why they're well-made and sturdy. As I recall, you still have two of your trucks and even though you played a lot with them, they are still in good condition."

And then we were at the shore of the lake.

"Dad," I said, "The lake is huge!" And Billy added that it is a big lake, and the Dakota word Minnetonka means "big water."

"It is the fourth largest lake in Minnesota and is perfect for boating and fishing in the summer. And, in the winter, the lake freezes, and you can ice skate and some people cut holes in the ice and fish."

"Sounds like fun, Dad. Can we swim or go boating today?"

"We will swim, fish, and go boating when we get to the Lake of the Woods near the end of our trip. Until then, remember this lake and all the lakes we will see on our trip north"

"Are we going to see all 10,000 lakes?" Drew asks.

I love my brother, but how do I explain that visiting all 10,000 lakes would take more than a lifetime?

CHAPTER 3

Vikings to America

We leave the shores of Lake Minnetonka and drive northwest, and dad says," We are now going to Alexandria, and we may see a Viking there."

Drew, whose mind is always busy, pipes up and says, "Vikings, are we going to see the Minnesota Vikings football team? That would be super fun!"

Dad and Billy could barely control themselves with laughter. "Well, the football team is named after the Vikings who sailed across the Atlantic Ocean to America over 1,000 years ago. Leif Eriksson and brave Vikings led these adventures. They established a settlement in Eastern Canada 500 years before Christopher Columbus sailed from Spain and landed in the West Indies in the Caribbean Ocean."

"Wait, if the Native Americans were here 9,000 to 12,000 years ago, then they were here before the Vikings and Columbus!" said

Drew with excitement.

"Excellent, Drew!" Billy said, "That is correct! And to continue the story about when the Vikings came to America, it is possible a small group of Vikings got in a smaller boat and traveled across the Great Lakes, down rivers and found their way to Alexandria, Minnesota, the next stop on our trip."

I thought to myself, the end of the Ice Age, Native Americans following animals from Siberia to North America, the Vikings crossing the Atlantic Ocean and landing in Canada. The journey of Native Americans and the advance of the Vikings was intriguing.

Billy saw our puzzled looks and tried to help us understand with some details, "The Vikings crossed the Atlantic Ocean and landed near Nova Scotia in the year 1350, and Christopher Columbus sailed from Spain and reached the Islands in the Caribbean in 1492."

Drew said, "So it was a race in old wooden ships to see who got here first?

Now I had to laugh. "Drew, let Billy continue."

Billy said, "The Viking countries are all along the Atlantic Ocean including Sweden, Norway, and Denmark. Living in cities by the ocean, the Vikings grew up sailing. They were very adventurous and not only sailed to other countries to trade goods, but they were also fierce fighters and had a long history of raiding towns and conquering lands."

Drew, always thinking, said, "And everyone who came here must have been thrilled to see so many lakes and I wonder if they knew how they were formed?"

"Ok" I said, "this is fascinating."

ALEXANDRIA
BIRTHPLACE OF
AMERICA

C H A P T E R 4

Alexandria, Big Ole and
the Runestone

On our drive to Alexandria, we passed many farms and Dad and Billy pointed out the crops in the fields.

Billy said, "See that field? That's wheat with its long stems and seed pods. Over there, you can see the farmer is growing sugar beets. And look over there; that is a cornfield with bright green leaves and golden tassels at the top of the stalks."

Billy continues, "Minnesota has rich farmland good for growing crops. The Vikings and their ancestors, your great grandparents, all came to Minnesota knowing they could grow crops and feed their families."

Drew shouts, "Look, a town is ahead of us. Is that Alexandria? Are we going to see Vikings?"

Dad says, "Yes, that is Alexandria. We will be there in a few minutes, and you may be surprised at what you will see."

As we enter the town, there is something huge at the end of

Main Street.

"There, there!" Drew exclaims. "Look, look, a Viking!!"

Both dad and Billy laugh out loud, and Billy explains. "What you see is Big Ole, America's biggest Viking. He is a 28-foot tall re-creation of a Viking. Do you think someone like him sailed across the Atlantic Ocean and found his way to Alexandria? We may never know, but that's part of a mystery surrounding a stone found here in Alexandria."

I know the Vikings were big and fierce, but not as big as Ole. That would be like the Jolly Green Giant, which is another Minnesota story.

We walk around Big Ole, marvel at his size and think about all the Vikings who traveled the world.

Dad says, "The next stop before dinner is the Runestone Museum, where we will see a large flat stone a farmer found in his field with Viking letters carved into it. The Viking letters are called Runes and since the carved letters in the stone are Runes, they call the stone the Runestone. Some say the stone was carved by that adventurous group of Vikings who traveled in a smaller boat from the East Coast of Canada across the Great Lakes and down rivers to Alexandria."

Billy, always one to keep us laughing with his wonderful Minnesota sense of humor, said, "You know, that farmer didn't leave any stone unturned."

Native Americans, Vikings, a Runestone, 10,000 lakes and now Big Ole—I think to myself—is this an education of multiple mysteries we must solve? I need to rest my brain!

No rest for us as I can see that dad is excited to show us the Runestone and head over to the museum where the Runestone is on display. Dad had already told us about the farmer who found the Runestone in his field one day and recognized that it had unusual writing. The Museum Director met us as we entered the Museum, and we learned that the farmer dug up the stone and brought it to Alexandria for everyone to see. The rune alphabet is peculiar with odd symbols and the mysterious history of the Runestone is still debated to this day.

Whether the Runestone is old or not, it is fun to learn about the Viking alphabet and language.

"I'm hungry," said Drew. And we all know what that means—time to go and leave history behind us.

Dad said, "Ok, enough history for one day. Let's find a local café and have dinner.

"Great idea," said Drew, "I can't wait to see what the Alexandria restaurants have to offer—maybe Viking food like big roasted turkey legs?"

CHAPTER 5

Mississippi River, Bemidji, and Paul Bunyan

We stayed overnight in Alexandria and the next morning; we got up early and had a super good breakfast with "Viking" pancakes large enough for Big Ole. We didn't know anything about our next stop, but we thought it had something to do with a river when Billy started talking about the Mississippi River while driving. But why was he talking about a river when we were supposed to solve the mystery of the lakes?

Billy said, "The Mississippi River starts in Minnesota and goes south to the Gulf of Mexico. It is one of the world's great rivers, the one Mark Twain wrote about in his adventures of Tom Sawyer and Huckleberry Finn. I'll bet you a dime I can walk across the Mississippi River."

Drew and I looked at each other. We knew Billy liked to tell funny stories, but there was no way he could walk across that wide river. On television at home in Arizona, we saw huge riverboats on the

Mississippi River, a wide, deep river. Surely, no one could walk across the river, so we took him up on his bet.

After about two hours and lots of thinking about how in the world Billy could walk across the river, he stopped the car, and we got out to stretch our legs. We walked a little way past an information center to a small footbridge crossing a little creek. Billy stopped before crossing it, looked back at us, smiled, and walked over the bridge. Then he gave us a knowing grin and said, "Okay, you both owe me a dime!"

We looked at each other and back at Billy. He and Dad were both laughing. Then we saw a sign near the footbridge that said this was the "headwaters" of the Mississippi River! It was a small creek where the river began and with Billy, all of us could walk across it. We stood at the beginning of the mighty river the Algonquin Indians had called the "great water."

Drew and I each gave Billy a dime, but then we ran across the bridge over the little stream. We figured when we got back to Arizona, we could boggle a lot of brains by telling our friends we had walked across the Mississippi River!

We got back into the car and drove to another lake to have a picnic lunch. Drew and I raced each other to the shore of Lake Bemidji, but as we got near the water, we stopped in our tracks. There stood two huge statues, one of a guy who looked like a lumberjack and another of a big cow. And the cow was blue!

"That's Paul Bunyan and his blue ox, Babe!" dad said. Then I remembered them, too. "Yeah," I said. "But they aren't real, Drew, they were, like, what do you call it dad?"

"A legend," dad said. "Sort of a folk tale people used to tell and pass along."

Drew's eyes were as big as saucers and he said "First, we have Big Ole, a giant Viking, and now Paul Bunyan and a Blue Ox? Minnesota is amazing and full of surprises."

Drew and I read the engraved plaque near the colorful statues. At first, we were excited because we thought we had solved the mystery of the 10,000 lakes—and even how the Mississippi River was formed. The legend was that Paul Bunyan, the greatest (and biggest) lumberjack of all time, created the Mississippi River; when tired from a long day's work of chopping down trees, he dragged his ax along the ground behind him. As the huge ax cut into the ground, a stream was formed and that was the beginning of the Mississippi River. And, as you already know, the Mississippi River begins here in Minnesota. As for the lakes, it is said that Babe, his blue ox, made the lakes one spring day when the ground was soft. Babe's huge hoofs left more than 10,000 holes in the ground all over the state, which filled with water and became the lakes.

Drew and I discussed it and decided that the "legend" of Paul

Bunyan and his blue ox was cool, but it wasn't the answer to the mystery.

After lunch, we piled back into the car and headed north. Here and there we would see a clearing where a section of forest had been turned into farmland. Drew and I noticed that many of the farm fields had huge piles of gray rocks.

"Where'd all those rock piles come from?" Drew asked. Dad smiled and said if we could figure that out, we could also figure out how all the lakes were formed. In other words, the rocks were a clue to the mystery of the 10,000 lakes or 15,291 lakes, according to Billy.

That night, we pitched a tent on the shore of a nearby lake, ate dinner, watched fireflies in the dark sky and fell asleep dreaming about Vikings, lumberjacks and a huge blue ox.

LAKE BRONSON DAM

River water level receded
In this drought, a lake is needed,
A concrete dam is conceived
Two Rivers water relieved.

A site is chosen
For the dam's location,
The river winks and agrees
A perfect spot beyond the trees.

A Natural elevation
To receive the formation,
All systems are go
For the dam to grow.

Concrete forms put in place
Mixing sand and gravel with grace,
Scaffolds begin to soar
Skyward from the river's floor.

Half way done
Shining in the sun,
Anticipation fills the air
Like opening day at the fair.

The end is near as seasons pass
Almost finished with the mass,
A prayer for all who make
The beautiful dam and lake.

Not far from the town
Lake Bronson Dam is fully grown,
Water cascades over the gait
All has been worth the wait.

Applause abounds from those gathered near
Farmers, friends and families cheer,
Kittson County is proud of the birth
Of the dam and lake from Mother Earth.

Randy Persson

LAKE
BRONSON

CHAPTER 6

Lake Bronson

My dad and Billy were born in Kittson County and grew up on their parents' farms. My dad grew up on a farm in Lake Bronson and Billy and his brothers and sister, grew up on a farm west of town on the road to Kennedy. Dad's family was Swedish and traced their family tree back to Southern Sweden. Dad told us that Grandma Ione's mother, Alma, was born in southern Sweden and, like many immigrants, she got passage on a ship to cross the Atlantic Ocean to America to seek a better life. She was a true present-day Viking. And Dad told us Great Grandma Alma cried when the vessel entered the New York harbor and she saw the Statue of Liberty.

Drive, drive, drive. More and more farmland. And, finally, when it seemed like we were at the end of the earth, we saw another small town with a giant grain elevator and a tall round water tower on top of long shiny steel legs.

Dad said with pride, "This is Lake Bronson. Welcome to my

hometown."

As we approached the town, Drew and I strained our necks to look out the car windows. First, we saw a huge grassy area with lots of old tractors and then we saw a row of trees and Dad stopped the car.

"This is the Kittson County Veterans Memorial to remember all those who fought in the armed services for our country. Let's get out of the car and walk around the memorial and I'll show you the bench dedicated to Grandpa Reuben with his name and three Purple Hearts etched into the granite."

And there it was—a beautiful granite bench with Grandpa Reuben's name on it.

Dad said, "Grandpa Reuben was in the Army and fought in World War II. He was deployed to the South Pacific where he fought in many battles and was wounded three times. He was shot twice, and one wound was from shrapnel that went into his leg. The doctors were afraid to dig it out because he might lose his leg if something went wrong, so he carried that shrapnel in his leg for the rest of his life. Each time he was wounded, the doctors wanted to send him home, but Grandpa said, 'patch me up. I've got to get back to my unit. My buddies need me to help fight.'"

We left the Veteran's memorial, crossed the bridge over the Twin Forks River and soon turned right onto Main Street. We passed a large and tall grain elevator, then over the railroad tracks and were in the middle of town. The main street was wide and there were no stoplights. Dad explained that only a few stores remained where there was once a bank, a bowling alley, a creamery where farmers sold their milk and a couple of restaurants. Now it was a smaller town and incredibly quiet.

As we drove slowly through town, dad pointed out the Farmers' store that sold about everything people needed, including groceries, clothing, and farm tools. Next was a restaurant where dad loved to eat the best hamburgers in the world. He said they were juicy and always made with a fresh bun right out of the oven. And then we saw the creamery where Grandpa Reuben sold milk from his cows. We were about out of town and dad stopped the car in front of the Kittson County Historical Museum.

We got out of the car and dad said we would go back in time to when pioneers first came to the area, and we may even learn about how the lakes were formed.

Cindy Adams, the Museum Director, met us as we entered the museum. She welcomed us and gave us a brief history of the museum. She said the best way to see the museum was to walk around, so we started down a journey into the history of Kittson County. We saw many things including information about the Native Americans who lived in the area, exhibits of tools and the sod houses used and built by the early pioneers.

Drew said, "Did the Vikings come here first or the Native Americans and what about the lake—why is the town called Lake Bronson and I don't see a lake?"

Dad and Billy looked at each other and I could tell they were trying to figure out how to answer Drew's questions.

Finally, Billy said, "Native American tribes were the first people to live in the area. Then came hunters and trappers and then the pioneers who settled here and farmed the land. The Vikings may have had a small boat and came down a river that passed through. They would have fished and hunted for food along the way before they finally stopped at Alexandria."

We all thoroughly enjoyed the fascinating museum—especially seeing the history of the area and learning about the land and the hardships of the pioneers who settled here.

We said goodbye to Cindy and got back in the car. We had not gone far down a dirt road when dad stopped the car and said, "this is the house grandpa and grandma built and where I grew up."

"Looks small," said Drew.

"Well," said dad, "it didn't seem small to me when I was your age. It was warm and cozy in the winter and with the creek just beyond the house, it was a beautiful place to look for minnows in the summer."

"Can we see the creek, Dad?" I asked.

"Yes, it's just beyond this grassy field and over here is where we had a huge garden. We grew vegetables like peas, cabbage, radishes, carrots, and corn. Nothing tastes better than fresh veg-

etables from the garden. I loved pulling a shiny green pea pod off

it's stem, popping it open and eating the fresh peas. So sweet

and tasty—not at all like peas we get today in a can. We also grew

rhubarb and strawberries. Grandma's rhubarb and strawberry pie

was the best. I loved her pie so much that one day I pulled off a

rhubarb stalk from the garden and bit into it. It was so sour I spat it

out and ran to the well to get a drink of water and wash the horrible

taste out of my mouth. Lesson learned, do not eat raw rhubarb."

Dad made the funniest face and we all laughed.

We walked down to the creek and dad showed us where he

caught little, tiny minnows. The small stream was cold, clear, and

beautiful, and we could see why dad loved living here.

Dad said. when he was seven years old, he got asthma and

the doctors told his parents to move to Arizona. He said he was

so sick that he was in the hospital in an oxygen tent and Grandpa

and Grandma hurried up and sold the house and the cows, pigs

and the farm equipment and off to Arizona they went.

"Ok," Dad said, "that's Lake Bronson, the town, and our farm.

Next is the real Lake Bronson and I know you will be interested to

learn how it was formed."

"Wait," said Drew," aren't WE supposed to solve the mystery

of the 10,000 lakes?"

CHAPTER 7

Lake Bronson – The Lake

We drove away from the farmhouse on a dirt road, across a bridge and over the creek. Just before we got to a highway, dad stopped that car. We all got out and dad said, "Look over there. That is the family farm." Grandpa Reuben grew corn, wheat, and oats until we moved to Arizona. Now it is in a government conservation program to preserve the soil. Ok, back in the car; next stop is Lake Bronson—the lake, and let's see how it was created."

The lake wasn't very far and when we got there, dad asked, "Does this lake look like all the other lakes we have seen?"

Drew said, "Well this one has a dam at one end and the others didn't."

"Very good Drew," said Billy, "And who do you think built the dam and why?"

"Ok," Drew said, "I'll bet it was beavers or those Vikings from Alexandria who came up the river and decided to build it."

Now it was my turn to smile and both dad and Billy laughed out loud.

Dad said, "The U.S. Government built this dam and when they dammed up the river, the lake was formed."

I asked, "Dad, did the government create the 10,000 lakes the same way?"

"Good question, Taylor. In the 1930s, believe it or not, even with all the rivers and lakes in Minnesota, there was a water shortage in this area, so the U.S. government built the dam on the Two Rivers to create the lake behind it. They trapped the water behind the dam so the people in the area would have water during the severe drought. Climates change and this is a good lesson on how we as humans must adapt."

"So," said Drew, "If the Vikings didn't build the dam, Babe the Blue Ox didn't create the lakes with her hoofprints, and the government built it, I'm lost. How were the other 10,000 lakes formed?"

Dad Looked at both of us and said, "I'm going to give you a clue. Do you remember we talked briefly about the Ice Age?"

I said, "Of course, that's when huge glaciers covered a large part of the earth and animals like mammoths and saber tooth tigers were migrating to warmer climates and the tribes were following them."

Dad continued, "Do you know that glaciers covered almost all of Minnesota? What do you think happened when the ice melted?"

Drew, being Drew, piped up, "That's a lot of ice and what about the animals that were here? Oh wait, I saw the movie "Ice Age" and Manny the Mammoth, Sid the Sloth and Diego the Saber Tooth Tiger were escaping from the melting ice. Is that what happened here?"

"Ok, that's the clue for the day. Let's set up camp in the Lake Bronson campground. I'll build a fire, fix dinner and we can roast marshmallows before we go to sleep. In the morning, we will drive to the Lake of the Woods and catch some fish on the biggest fresh-water lake in the United States—a massive lake that stretches from Minnesota to Canada."

CHAPTER 8

Lake Of the Woods

We got up early and dad fixed fluffy round pancakes with butter and maple syrup. After breakfast, we got in the car and after about an hour, Dad said, "The Lake of the Woods is over 70-miles wide and long. It is the sixth largest freshwater lake in the United States after the five Great Lakes. This is where Grandpa Reuben and Uncle Grant, took me and cousins Billy and Gary fishing each summer. This trip was the highlight of our summer, and we couldn't wait to get there."

We drove for a long time and finally passed some signs that we were near the Lake of the Woods and kept going. Suddenly Drew almost yelled through the roof, "Dad! Dad! There, look there! A Viking fish as big as a house!! Wow!!!"

Dad and Billy laughed out loud and yes; it was a giant fish. Billy said, "We are now in Baudette, Minnesota, the Walleye Capital of the World."

Billy continued and said, "That's Willie the Walleye. Willie is over 40-feet long and weighs around 2 ½ tons. Yup, one big fish. Do you think you might catch one like him?"

Billy was a funny guy, and I could see the concern on Drew's face at trying to catch a fish that big, but I wasn't going to say a word.

Dad stopped the car; we got out and dad said that Grandpa Reuben had indeed caught a large walleye on the lake many years ago but not that big. He told us that Willie was built by the local town residents as a tribute to the type of fish found in the Lake and to remind people that there is excellent fishing here.

Drew finally got it and chuckled and was relieved to know he wouldn't have to catch a fish that big.

It was nearing sunset, so we checked into a motel for the night dreaming of all the fish we would catch the next day.

None of us got much sleep that night because we were so excited to go fishing. As soon as the sun came up, we got in the car and headed down to the dock on the lake.

We all had to get fishing licenses at the fishing shack and then dad rented a boat and fishing gear for the day. He also bought a large metal container of minnows we would use as bait. We headed out to one of dad's favorite fishing spots near Steelhead Point and fished all morning and afternoon. We caught a couple of walleyes, not nearly as big as Willie the Walleye but looked just like him. We also caught a fish called a sauger, which is like a walleye but smaller. We had so much fun on this vast, beautiful lake. I can see why Grandpa Reuben and Great Uncle Grant, made this annual trip.

Finally, we called it a day and reluctantly headed back to the dock. We turned in the boat and the fishing gear and put the fish we had caught in an ice chest. Then, as tired and excited as I have ever been, we got in the car and started driving east down the highway away from Lake of The Woods.

After a few miles, Dad said, "Now you have seen many lakes and my hometown, plus the rich Viking and Scandinavian history, yet we haven't solved the mystery of the 10,000 lakes."

Dad continued, "One last clue is that the glaciers that covered this land in the Ice Age did melt and the water from the melting ice had to go somewhere. Think about that as we drive to Duluth on the western edge of Lake Superior."

"Dad," said Drew, "I don't want to leave. I love it here. Can't we do more exploring and fishing? Can we go back to Lake Bronson and fish some more? This is fun!"

Dad smiled and said, "I have one more surprise for you. I know you like exploring and fishing, but do you like handmade candies?"

We both said at the same time, "Yes, we love candy! Do we

have some in the car?"

And I thought, okay, what does candy have to do with fishing and the mystery of 10,000 lakes?

And then, the surprise, we had driven for about three hours, and it was nearing dinner time. We were all getting hungry, but the thought of chocolate was the only dinner on our minds.

Finally, we stopped in a town called Virginia. Not the state on the east coast of the United States but a city in Minnesota.

And on the sign in front of this store said *Canelake's Candies, established 1905.*

Wowzer, who cares about fishing? Let's go.

It turns out, dad has a good friend whose family opened Canelake's Candies almost 120 years ago, and for four generations, the family has been making yummy candies in giant copper kettles. According to dad, they make the best candy in the world—or at least the United States!

Ok, this is fun. One of the owners, Chris Canelake, was there and welcomed us in. The air was full of such sweet smells.

"This is heaven!" said Drew and we all laughed.

Chris took us to the kitchen where caramels, chocolates, toffees, and fudge were cooking. The candy kitchen cooks gave us samples of different candies and although we could have stayed there all night, we did need to get to our hotel and have some dinner—or not!

Chris boxed up our favorite candies, said goodbye, and we headed to our hotel for one last night in Minnesota.

CHAPTER 9

Lake Superior

We got up early, checked to make sure our candy boxes were there, got in the car and dad said "Our next and last stop in Minnesota is the town of Duluth and Lake Superior. Lake Superior is one of the Great Lakes between the United States and Canada and is huge, even bigger than Lake of the Woods. It is the largest freshwater lake in the world!"

Dad paused to let us think about how big the lake must be and then continued, "You have had a chance to travel across Minnesota and see many lakes, and I have to ask you—how do you think all the lakes were formed? Certainly, the Vikings didn't dig the lakes and, yet they are all over Minnesota!"

Drew said, "The lakes are too big to have been dug by Vikings, even if they were the size of Big Ole or lumberjacks as big as Paul Bunyan and Babe the Blue Ox. Aliens! It had to be aliens who came here in their starships after the Ice Age and used gamma rays and lasers and stuff to create the lakes."

Well, you can't say Drew doesn't have an imagination—especially after seeing Big Ole, Paul Bunyan, and Willie the Walleye!!!

We sat quietly, thinking about the lakes as we arrived at Duluth. We drove by many buildings and finally, Billy stopped the car. We got out of the car and we saw blue water stretching as far as we could see. A few more steps and we saw water splashing on the breakwater and then a tall, beautiful lighthouse pointing skyward. And beyond the lighthouse, in the distance, we saw the biggest lake we have ever seen. It was so huge that it looked more like an ocean than a lake. It was Lake Superior, indeed the biggest lake of them all.

We all stood there with a cool soft wind coming of the lake and dad said. "We are at the end of our journey and now it's time to figure out how these lakes were formed. Taylor, what do you think?"

I said, "Well, you told us about the Ice Age, and we saw mounds of stones in unusual places in Minnesota. When the ice melted and the glaciers moved across the land, did the water go to the low areas and leave the stones behind?"

Drew, pretty smart for a little kid, jumped up and down and said, "Dad, dad, I know, I know."

Dad and Billy looked at him, and I'm thinking here we go again with the aliens.

"Ice is heavy, right? And the gigantic glaciers moved north as they melted, right? They must have torn up the earth like giant bulldozers as they moved and left holes in it and mounds of dirt and stones."

Oh, my goodness, Drew was on to something.

Dad and Billy looked at each other and smiled.

"Yes, Drew," Billy said. "As the glaciers melted, they did move north, and they left holes in the earth as they receded. These ancient glaciers tore into the rock surfaces and bulldozed basins that hold the lakes themselves. Large boulders and rock debris were carried along by the ice and were left behind as the climate warmed. And Lake Superior was formed as the ice mass moved north to form not only Lake Superior, but all the lakes we now see in Minnesota. Depending on the rocks the ice traveled over and scoured with its mass, you have seen lakes that are small holes and some that are gigantic like Lake of the Woods and Lake Superior."

Drew and I both felt like we not only had the trip of a lifetime—but we also learned a lot about Minnesota, the climate changing back in the Ice Age, Vikings, the headwaters of the Mississippi River, toys in Lake Minnetonka and so much more.

Dad said, "Another mystery of nature solved and another wonderful trip for all of us. Just remember Minnesota is the home of 10,000 beautiful lakes created by mother nature and carved out of the land by glaciers."

What an incredible trip. Mystery solved. Saying goodbye to Lake Superior, we got back in the car we drove south to the Twin Cities on the final leg of our trip. Our adventure was over until the next time!!!